ALL
SORTS of
Clothes

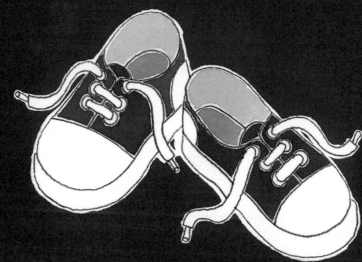

Picture Window Books
5115 Excelsior Boulevard
Suite 232
Minneapolis, MN 55416
877-845-8392
www.picturewindowbooks.com

Printed in the United States of America.

First published by Zero to Ten (a member of the Evans Publishing Group)
2A Portman Mansions, Chiltern Street, London, W1U 6NR, United Kingdom.

Copyright © Zero to Ten 2002
Text Copyright © Hannah Reidy 1999
Illustrations Copyright © Emma Dodd 1999
This edition published under license from Evans Brothers Limited.
All rights reserved.

Library of Congress Cataloging-in-Publication Data
Reidy, Hannah.
All sorts of clothes / written by Hannah Reidy ; illustrated by Emma Dodd.
p. cm. — (All sort of things)
Summary: Describes a variety of different clothes that children wear, such as a soft sweatshirt, a frilly dress, and a baseball cap.
ISBN 1-4048-1063-3 (hardcover)
[1. Clothing and dress—Fiction.] I. Dodd, Emma, 1969- ill. II. Title. III. Series.
PZ7.R27977Alsc 2004
[E]—dc22
2004023873

For Fay Hillier, e.d.

For Eoin. h.r.

ALL SORTS of Clothes

Written by Hannah Reidy
Illustrated by Emma Dodd

Special thanks to our reading consultant:
Susan Kesselring, M.A.
Literacy Educator
Rosemount-Apple Valley-Eagan (Minnesota) School District

PICTURE WINDOW BOOKS
Minneapolis, Minnesota

Becky loves her
checkered shirt.
She wears it when
she's working.

Cody's furry
collar keeps
him nice
and warm.

Owen loves his
buzzy bee suit.

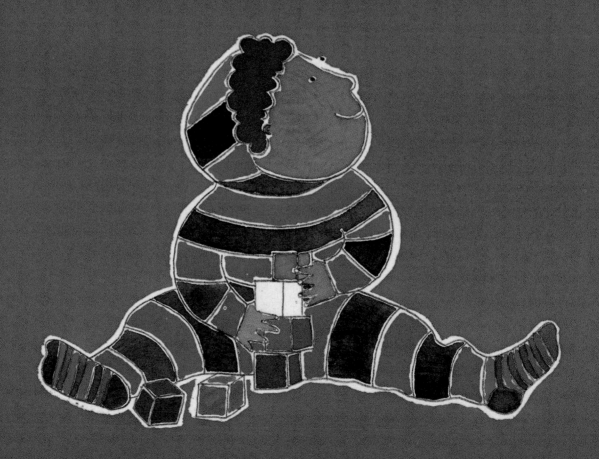

Oscar
prefers his
BIG BOY
clothes.

Isaac doesn't like his
itchy sweater.

He'd rather wear his **soft** sweatshirt.

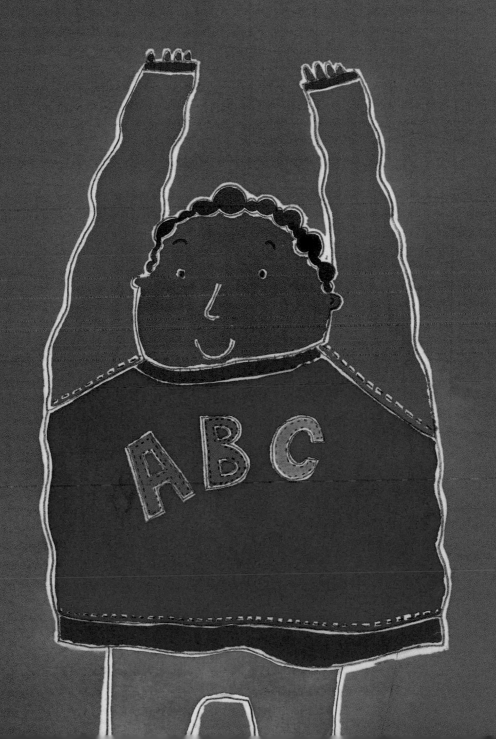

Louise wears
her **lacy**
dress for
parties.

Louie
wears his
ruffled
shirt.

Luke's
baseball cap
looks **cool** with
his Dad's new
sunglasses.

Patty has
lots of pockets
on her striped
overalls.

Toby's **teddy**
pajamas are
soft and **warm**
and perfect
for dreaming.

What do you like to wear?

FUN FACTS

- Athletes first used sweatshirts while warming up before sports or to stay warm after playing. The sweatshirts were gray.

- Baseball players started wearing the visor caps worn by Civil War soldiers. These caps eventually became baseball caps.

- When your head is exposed to cold, you can lose 70 percent of your body heat.

- The first pair of sunglasses was created in 1752.

- Many sweaters are made of wool. Wool comes from sheep.

WORDS TO KNOW

checkered—something that has a pattern of colored blocks

collar—the part of a shirt or coat that goes around your neck

furry—having fur or fabric that feels like fur; hairy

itchy—anything that tickles or scratches your skin

lacy—something with fine threads that make fancy designs

overalls—pants that fit loosely, cover the chest, and have suspenders

striped—something that has a pattern of lines on it

TO LEARN MORE

At the Library

Calmenson, Stephanie. *The Principal's New Clothes*. New York: Scholastic, 1989.

Gunzi, Christiane. *My Very First Look at Clothes*. Chanhassen, Minn.: Two-Can, 2003.

Johansen, Heidi Leigh. *My Clothes*. New York: PowerKids Press, 2005.

Wade, Barrie. *The Emperor's New Clothes*. Minneapolis: Picture Window Books, 2004.

On the Web

FactHound offers a safe, fun way to find Web sites related to this book.

All of the sites on FactHound have been researched by our staff.

www.facthound.com

   1. Visit the FactHound home page.

   2. Enter a search word related to this book, or type in this special code: 1404810633

   3. Click on the FETCH IT button.

Your trusty FactHound will fetch the best Web sites for you!

23

INDEX

baseball cap, 15, 22

collar, 7, 22

dress, 12

overalls, 17, 22

pajamas, 19

shirt, 5, 13, 22

suit, 8

sunglasses, 15, 22

sweater, 10, 22

sweatshirt, 11, 22

Look for all of the books in the All Sorts of Things series:

All Sorts of Clothes

All Sorts of Noises

All Sorts of Numbers

All Sorts of Shapes